9 BEST KEPT SECRETS

of B2B

DIGITAL MARKETING

Digital Marketing Strategies for Executives and Sales Managers

GREG GUTKOWSKI

9 Best Kept Secrets of B2B Digital Marketing
Digital Marketing Strategies for Executives and Sales Managers

Greg Gutkowski

ISBN: 978-0692499788
Published by: B2B Strategies, LLC

Praise for The 9 Best-Kept Secrets of B2B Digital Marketing

"Greg's book offers a lot of great advice that will save you a lot of money and frustration while implementing B2B digital marketing programs."

Jack Porter-Smith
Top Contributor, Google AdWords
Managing Director, WSI Paid Search Ltd.

"Relevant, simple, ESSENTIAL! Greg Gutkowski offers insight and advice that no one in the B2B community can afford to ignore. This book takes the mystery out of online marketing and puts the tools and resources in the hands of those responsible for driving revenue. I really appreciate Greg's ability to showcase the collaborative impact of traditional and online marketing strategies in a practical and cost-effective way. B2B companies and their sales teams will benefit from the knowledge garnered in these pages."

Katina Phillips,
Vice President and Business Banking Officer, BBVA Compass

"In an ever-increasingly crowded and confusing digital world, Greg Gutkowski takes the complexity out of the B2B marketing world and distills it down to a handful of digestible and executable steps for success. Very well worth reading!"

Rachid Zahidi,
Best-selling author
CEO, Sentinel Background Checks

Greg's book has written a very usable book for B2B executives who may be intrigued or frustrated with digital marketing. I can hear business leaders sighing with relief after reading and applying the 9 best-kept secrets in Greg's book."

Joe Yazbeck,
Founder and President, Prestige Leadership Advisors
International Speaker and Coach
Author of the best-selling book *No Fear Speaking*

"Greg Gutkowski provides actionable recommendations throughout the book, all supported with case studies. He outlines the problem(s), states the solutions, and describes the results. The book is an easy and very useful read."

Adel I. El-Ansary,
Professor of Marketing, Coggin College of Business, University of North Florida

"A must-read for every B2B manager and a wake-up call to everyone who has business responsibilities in a B2B environment. We all know digital marketing is here to stay and has become very relevant. This book provides clear direction for any B2B manager wanting to gain the most from their marketing efforts."

Reinaldo Campos,
Entrepreneur, International Business Development

FOREWORD

Effective marketing is always evolving. If you want to keep up and create lasting success you must evolve with it. Technology has forced the business to consumer relationship in to an entirely new paradigm and now businesses are being forced to relate the same way.

Globalization may be bringing us altogether, but it is also demanding more and more creativity to get your message out and your brand recognized. As competition and technology move the bar ever higher, digital marketers have had to reinvent themselves over and over again just to keep up. In fact, whole business models have had to be redesigned and replaced.

In this book, "9 Best Kept Secrets of B2B Digital Marketing", Greg Gutkowski helps businesses recognize and define these important shifts in the marketplace and apply new and highly effective ideas (his secrets) for business to business marketing.

You will find this an easy and straightforward read, something I know as a 30 year marketing professional who has read just about everything on selling, you will appreciate.

~Chris Gibson

Chris Gibson is an internationally known best-selling author and respected holistic health and lifestyle expert. He has sold over million books and is regularly featured on radio and television.

PREFACE

If you recognize any of these frustrations, this book is for you:

- You are running a successful B2B business and until now you did not have to worry about digital marketing.

- You sense you need to do something but do not know where to start.

- You may not know how much money you should allocate to your digital presence.

- You wonder if you have to blog, tweet, have friends on Facebook, engage on LinkedIn, and rank on the first page of a Google search.

- You are irked by digital marketing jargon, hype, mixed messages, and the lack of transparency from the Internet titans.

- You wonder if you have to keep up with digital Joneses.

- You marvel at the astonishing rate of technological change but wonder how long you can keep up with it.

- **You ask yourself what kind of marketing advice you may be getting from a 30-something expert with a lax dress code and no experience in your business.**

In less than 10 years, two young Stanford graduates conquered the world with Google. Now, they lead one of the largest companies globally. It has revolutionized advertising, searching, and analytics. A new verb was even added to our vocabulary – to "Google" something. At the same time, Facebook has signed up over one billion users around the world!

Billion dollar fortunes have been made on the Internet, yet many fortunes have been lost by business leaders who have been blindsided by the rapidly changing technologies. Printing businesses, travel bureaus, the music and book publishing industries, distributors, services, manufacturing, transportation, and software companies as well as news organizations are among those deeply impacted by the Internet. You may be wondering what side of the equation your business is on.

TABLE OF CONTENTS

INTRODUCTION

This is not an academic textbook. It's not a do-it-yourself manual either. It's a collection of unbiased business tips based on my extensive experience with Internet technologies, data analytics, sales management, and digital marketing. I hope that revealing these 9 secrets will save you a lot of money and frustration.

Digital marketing is a blend of traditional, timeless marketing concepts coupled with rapidly changing Internet technologies, technical creativity, and lots of analytics. The unprecedented progress in digital technologies is mainly responsible for the new ways of achieving ageless goals: introducing new products, selling them, and keeping customers happy.

To illustrate the power and price points of modern information and telecommunication technologies, let's use the iPhone as an example. It's a mini-computer that would have cost $3.5 million 20 years ago and was the size of your living room. The Apollo mission that landed us on the moon was supported by a fraction of an iPhone's computing power.

The endless increase in computing power coupled with decreasing software prices made it feasible (both technically and financially) to perform an unimaginable number of detailed transactions spanning the world. This enormous amount of data (Big Data) can be stored and analyzed at a very low cost. We are in the midst of a measurement revolution, leading to more effective and more efficient ways of achieving marketing goals.

Traditional marketers have seldom been technologists or data analysts, so I wrote this book to bridge the chasm between traditional marketing and its modern digital cousin. This book offers advice to B2B executives on how much to invest in their digital presence and how to allocate the resources among various digital alternatives. It also discusses the need for data integration for seamless real time analytics, leading to better resource allocation. I promise straight talk as I am associated with no technology vendor.

The cost of ignoring B2B digital marketing can be substantial. You may not go out of business tomorrow if you are not being found on the Internet today. However, you will be slowly losing business to more knowledgeable competitors.

You may be missing the opportunity to grow your business with a reasonable investment. You can't expect your B2B business to go viral due to digital marketing; however, a well-executed digital marketing program can grow your business by 15–20 percent every year.

This book illustrates how digital marketing impacts your whole organization. I'll discuss branding, PR, sales management, promotions, customer service, and IT challenges in the context of ever-changing Internet technologies.

Digital marketing is less expensive compared to print, radio, television, or hiring a new salesperson. Actually, it's the least expensive way to grow your business. So, let me show you how!

"The spread of computers and the Internet will put jobs in two categories. People who tell computers what to do, and people who are told by computers what to do."
—Marc Andreessen

"Try to learn something about everything and everything about something."
—Thomas Huxley

FACTS AND FADS

B2B Digital Marketing – What It Is and Isn't

The traditional definition of marketing is still very relevant. It includes coordination of the 4 Ps:

- Development of a *product*

- Setting its *price*

- Selection of distribution to reach a customer's *place*

- Development and implementation of *promotions*

Digital marketing is nothing more than using Internet and telecommunication technologies to manage the four Ps. These technologies are the most relevant to distribution and promotions. For example, a distribution may be an e-commerce store, and promotion may take the form of a paid advertisement on Google.

This does not mean that the digital ways are at the exclusion of traditional ones. On the contrary, they should work and support each other. E-commerce sites may coexist with a network of traditional distributors. Paid advertising on Google does not exclude promoting businesses during traditional trade shows. Posting on social networks can complement a handwritten "thank you" note.

As illustrated in the picture below, a digital marketing framework is based on your website and four digital channels supporting traditional marketing channel:

- **Search**

- **Email**

- **Paid ads**

- **Social media**

DIGITAL MARKETING FRAMEWORK PUSH AND PULL

Website – Pull

Your website is the heart of your Internet presence. A good website has the following attributes:

- **Informs about your products and company**

- **Is easy to use**

- **Can easily be found when your products are searched on the Internet (attracts the right visitors and pulls them in)**

- **Converts visitors to prospects or customers (by calling or filling out a form)**

- **Collects as many email addresses from visitors as possible**

- **Makes money for you (in the case of e-commerce sites)**

Most B2B websites today exhibit only the first attribute. They are nice electronic business cards collecting digital dust because few can be found.

Search – Pull

You need to be found easily on the Internet when a prospective customer is looking for your product. You need to pull your prospects to your website. There is a set of techniques called Search Engine Optimization, or SEO, to accomplish that goal. They are based on the concept of matching what a prospective customer types into Google with what is described on your website. For example, if a prospective customer enters "shower door manufacturer" in a Google search, and you are in the shower door business, it would be desirable for your website to be listed on the first page of results. More discussion of this concept can be found in Secret 1.

Email – Push

Email is a great way to stay in touch with existing customers and prospects that shared their email with you on your website. Email does not get all the media attention, but it's a very effective way to push your message out on a periodic basis. More on that topic in Secret 3.

Paid Ads – Push and Pull

Paid ads may be displayed when a prospect is searching for you in Google – this will be a form of a "pull." However, paid ads can also be displayed when prospects are visiting media sites and your product is complementary to the theme of an article they read. For example, when someone is reading about air quality, an ad about clear air monitoring equipment is "pushed" next to the article. More insights on paid ads follow in Secret 8.

Social Media – Push and Pull

Social media serves a dual role as far as pulling and pushing your message out. You may be posting/pushing messages on many social media sites in order to pull some visitors to your own social media site and/or blog. We discuss social media for B2B in depth in Secret 7.

Digital Glue

The digital marketing framework is glued together by the relevant and consistent content flowing among all channels doing the pushing and pulling. We need to assure conceptual as well as graphical consistency on all fronts of our Internet presence.

The digital currency of Internet marketing includes specific keywords describing your products and services (more discussion on this subject follows in Secret 1). These keywords have to be present on your website, and in your emails, social media posts, and paid ads.

Digital Marketing Is Not for Me

Executives from successful B2B organizations frequently tell me:

"We have built our business on traditional marketing, word-of-mouth, and direct sales. We are doing just fine."

"What is all this blogging, tweeting, and Facebooking going to get us?"

"I need to have my salespeople knocking on doors, making calls, and making things happen. We do not sell over the Internet."

Perception is reality. As a result, these successful B2B companies may not take advantage of the latest and greatest things happening in digital marketing. I think that part of the problem is a misunderstanding about the role of digital marketing in B2B enterprises.

B2B Versus B2C

The media is full of stories about successful Internet entrepreneurs young and old, as well as established companies making millions on the Internet. Most of the media coverage about digital marketing relates to pure-play Internet B2C companies whose revenues come from transactions made exclusively on the Internet. Other than e-commerce, they have no inventory or supply chain. Few of them have direct sales forces and corporate buyers. These are entertainment, media, and social media companies providing online gaming, e-learning, and web-based or cloud software services.

The media is guilty of abusing buzzwords and hyping things while using impenetrable digital marketing jargon. Very few of these stories are relevant to B2B, yet they dominate the coverage of digital marketing. B2B executives have reason to be skeptical.

Mastery of digital marketing in B2B is not a matter of survival as it is for B2C Internet companies. A mastery of digital media is not going to increase B2B revenue ten-fold in one year. However, digital marketing is the least expensive way to increase B2B revenues in the range of up to 20 percent per year. Therefore, digital marketing should play an important role in supporting the traditional pillars of revenue generation, such as a direct sales force, trade shows, and word of mouth.

Finding New Distributors

The best digital marketing return on investment (ROI) comes from having your B2B website catch buying signals from corporate/wholesale buyers looking for better deals on the Internet. Today, most B2B websites are not tuned up for such interceptions.

So, when a potential distributor looks for a good deal on a particular product and types "Product A" in a Google search, most producers of Product A do not show up. Thus, they are invisible to a potential wholesaler. The business will most likely be awarded to someone who showed up in Google search results.

A wholesaler is not expecting to buy Product A on the Internet; however, they expect to be able to find relevant, good quality information on the product along with a phone number for the rep. They may fill out a simple form if they want to be contacted at a later time.

How many sales leads are missed and how much revenue is lost depends on the company. However, catching leads resulting in signing up just five new distributors may mean a lot of new business.

Big Ticket Items

Some B2B companies offer products/services where a single sale may result in revenue well over $200,000. This is common among engineering firms, construction companies, enterprise software providers, environmental remediation services, and manufacturers of heavy equipment.

There may not be many searches on the Internet for these products and services. However, if someone is searching for a specific big ticket item costing $500K, it's more likely to be a highly motivated potential buyer as compared to a digital "tire kicker" doing price checks on commodity products. Just a couple of leads per year that turn into new business may pay for services of the best digital marketing agency.

Due Diligence

Whether you are looking for new distributors or direct buyers of large items, your website must stand up to close examination. Buyers will take the first steps to do due diligence on your business. If they land on a hard-to-use site with little relevant information, the likelihood of getting them engaged goes to zero.

Thus, you face two challenges. The first one is to be found by tuning your website to the buying signals. The second is to keep your visitor engaged after they've found you. The best way to achieve the second objective is to provide as much information in a relevant format in as few clicks as possible via the fast loading site (i.e. fact sheets, videos, PDF downloads, testimonials, and contact details).

Social Media for B2B

Unlike consumer-based businesses, B2B does not rely much on social media, however, a B2B company needs to have Twitter, LinkedIn, and Google+ basic professional profiles for due diligence by potential customers. Monitoring social media posts by competitors, customers, and partners may provide a wealth of market research and competitive intelligence information. More on this subject can be found in Secret 3.

DRIVING FORCES
What Drives Profound Changes in Marketing

Before we reveal the 9 secrets of B2B digital marketing, let's examine the major drivers behind the relentless technological change in marketing technologies:

- **Decreased prices for computing hardware, telecommunications, and software**

- **Explosion in software functionalities**

- **Cost of knowledgeable workers**

These phenomena working in concert are responsible for the neck-breaking pace of change affecting all aspects of marketing.

Decrease in Price of Computing Hardware

The table below illustrates the dramatic decrease in price of computing hardware between 1991 and 2014.

	1991	2014
1 GB of hard disk storage	$10,000.00	$0.04
1 GB of flash memory	$45,000.00	$0.55

In 23 years, the prices of computing hardware went down 10,000 times! I know of no other prices in human history that came down as much in such a short period of time.

A new Chevy Corvette 23 years ago was about $30K, if we used a 10K divider it would cost about $3 today, and a million dollar home would cost only $100.

The capabilities of computing power are improving at exponential rates. Gordon Moore, co-founder of Intel Corporation, predicted in 1965 that the capabilities of computing hardware would double every two years. He was right, and this trend has continued for more than half a century.

Decrease in Price of Telecommunications

There has been a corresponding decrease in the prices of telecommunications. It would be unthinkable 20 years ago to watch Netflix movies on a Wi-Fi connected tablet at home. The networks would be way too slow, and the cost would be completely prohibitive.

As the following table illustrates, an average iPhone would have cost $3.5 million only 23 years ago.

	1991	2014
Mid-level iPhone with 32GB flash memory + telecommunication package	$3,500,000	$350.00

Decreasing prices of software and hardware made cloud software services possible. Cloud services are based on a very compelling value proposition. Instead of installing and maintaining software and hardware at your office, subscribe to the identical functionality hosted on remote servers and accessible via the Internet (with nothing to install) at a fraction of the cost.

This model is especially attractive to smaller companies who do not have, or cannot afford, a dedicated IT professional to install and maintain hardware and software.

Decrease in Price of Software

Cloud-based services brought about professional grade software solutions at very low price points. In the past, only large companies could afford to buy and install expensive hardware and software at their premises as telecommunication prices were prohibitive. Software companies charged millions per installation because their costs were spread among very few customers. This expensive software provided a competitive advantage as smaller players could not afford it.

Not anymore. The power of software and hardware got democratized. Cloud software companies can now charge much less per user as they can access a much larger user base worldwide. Anyone can afford world class CRM (Customer Relationship Management) for $20 per user per month. What used to cost millions is now very inexpensive.

Explosion in Software Functionalities

The proliferation of less expensive but more powerful computers energized the software development community and unleashed a wave of creativity that has not subsided yet. What was unthinkable just a few years before became not only possible technically but could also make a software designer a fortune.

Perfect examples include 3-D animation brought to us by Pixar, super realistic video games, and streamed video services, such as Netflix.

On the marketing side, we are observing a proliferation of software packages that combine a wide variety of functionality under one "roof." The most recent examples include marketing automation packages that provide fully integrated functionalities, such as:

- **Lead generation and tracking**

- **Existing customer relationship management**

- **Social media engagement and monitoring**

- **Email marketing**

- **Landing page creation**

- **Search engine optimization**

- **Web traffic analysis and reporting**

- **Sales analysis and reporting**

Just a couple of years ago, each of the functionalities were available as separate expensive packages from various vendors. Imagine how time consuming it was to coordinate these packages and how much time could be saved by using an integrated system.

Cost of Knowledgeable Workers

In many companies, the cost of professionals is its single largest ongoing expense. Professionals are also its best asset. Increasing their productivity is of great importance.

Well-designed software may have a fundamental impact on the productivity of workers. Imagine financial\marketing analysis without an electronic spreadsheet, a sales rep without a cell phone, or a search without Google. At the end of the day, good technology serves only one purpose: to do the same task in less time.

GOOD NEWS – BAD NEWS

Good:

- There is a lot of technology to help you do things faster, better, and cheaper.

- We can collect a great deal of granular data, allowing for better analysis and resource allocation.

- There is a level playing field with respect to digital technologies regardless of the business size.

- The new marketing technologies are more effective and less expensive.

Bad:

- There are so many choices, ideas, and new products that it's a full-time job keeping up with them.

- There is a shortage of analytical skills in the market.

- A level playing field drives up the competition.

- Traditional marketers are not known for being technologists or data analysts.

9 BEST KEPT SECRETS OF B2B DIGITAL MARKETING

SECRET 1
BASIC HYGIENE
Getting Found in a Digital Haystack

Traditional B2B marketing involved, among other things, word of mouth, cultivating personal relationships, participation in trade shows, printing glossy brochures, print advertising, as well as direct selling by a captive sales force. I see no need for any of these methods to go away soon. However, all of them can be turbocharged by Internet technology.

Turbocharging the Traditional

Personal relationships can be enhanced by social media, especially via LinkedIn and Facebook. Participation in trade shows may be preceded by a creative email and/or social media campaign, resulting in a lot of traffic to your booth. Twitter can be used to monitor opinions of key trade show participants expressed during the convention. Social media chatter around trade shows can generate ideas for another creative follow up email campaign, resulting in a lot of post-show traffic to your website.

Brochures can still be printed. However, their content can be very well synchronized with the various pages on your website, so web traffic analysis can tell us what brochure or message was the most popular.

Your salespeople can leverage social media for lead generation, competitive intelligence, and customer service. Last, but not least, your website should be providing qualified leads to your sales force. Most B2B websites are not doing that today. They are just pretty electronic business cards sitting idle and not working for you.

So, the more things change, the more they remain the same. Principles of marketing and sales are not changing. What's changing very fast are the Internet technologies.

The Marvel of the Internet Search

One of these fascinating technologies, the Internet search, is responsible for the existence of Google, a company who built a $60 billion business in just 10 years by mastering the art of sifting through a staggering amount of information on the web. By the way, Google did not invent this technology – it just had a vision to marry it with advertising to people who search on the Internet.

The principle of this technology is quite simple. You type a name of something you are looking for, hit "Enter," and search engines go out to the cybersphere to bring you all the relevant information from websites and social media posts. Search engines return information as a list of results. These normally include a list of web pages with titles, a link to the full website page, and a short description of the website page. The top three positions on the first page are reserved for websites whose owners have purchased ads. The rest of the listings show up organically – with the best website at the top. You click on the link, and you land on a page containing information you were looking for.

Any Google search results in thousands of pages of listings being returned. However, few people have the time and energy to visit even the second page of these results. This is why Tony Soprano is known for saying that the best place to hide a dead body is on the second page of Google.

Hence, the competition to be found (or ranked) on the first page of Google.

Is It Really for Me?

You may be asking yourself this question: "Do people in my industry really search for my products or services?" The probability that people search for your type of products or services is almost 100 percent.

Corporate buyers come and go, and new companies are born, so even with the best network and sales people you cannot be everywhere and know about everybody who may be interested. This is especially true for any B2B company that operates in a national and international arena. You may be surprised to learn how many people are looking for things that you provide.

The top three search engines – Google, Bing, and Yahoo – store all searches performed on their sites. In other words, one can find how many times per year people were looking for "wholesale garden fertilizer," for example. Also, we know where the searches came from in terms of geography as well as the type of device used – desktop, smartphone, or tablet. In addition, we know how the number of searches fluctuated over time. This tells us about the peak demand for a product/service during a year.

Any reputable digital marketing agency will be able to do such an analysis for you.

How Does It Work?

Let's assume that people are searching for you. This brings about the second question: "Do I have a chance of being found on the first page?"

Your chances depend on two major factors:

1. **The technical structure and relevant content of your website**

2. **The competition from sites who also wish to rank on the first page**

If you do not meet the first criteria, you have next to no chance of ranking on the first page.

To have a chance of ranking on the first page, you have to meet approximately 12 technical criteria as established by Google and other search engines. In addition, Google wants to see your total devotion to your industry. How do they assess it? By analyzing how many times specific industry terms show up in your web copy. So, if you are a manufacturer of natural garden fertilizer, that exact phrase needs to be present on your web pages. Thus, if someone searches for natural garden fertilizer, Google can make a match and present your website to a web surfer who wants to tend to his or her garden.

Meeting the first criteria does not guarantee ranking at the very top. Everything else being equal, Google is giving you credit for the number and quality of links to your site from other websites as well. The more links you have (and the better they are), the more likely you are to be perceived as a legitimate business. For example, links from educational and government sites carry much more weight than links from your friend's website.

The rules and techniques described above are also referred to as Search Engine Optimization or SEO.

There is good news for B2B companies. It is much easier to rank for B2B products and services than for consumer businesses. There is a lot more competition for hotels or flowers than there is for aluminum fabrication or wholesale garden fertilizer. The more specifically your products and services are named, the easier it will be to have them found and ranked.

To Find and To Be Found

You need to generate more business. You can do it by finding new deals or being found by a prospective buyer. Your sales force is in charge of finding new deals. At the same time, your website should be in charge of corporate buyers finding you. Finding and being found should be closely coordinated.

The concept of being found is not new. The Yellow Pages made a lot of money from companies who wanted to be found before their competition was. In order to do that, they were buying full-page ads with a phone number prominently displayed in bold at the top. Less resourceful competitors had to do with less effective quarter-page listings. The more things change, the more they stay the same...

Most B2B companies rely on their network of wholesalers, distributors, and resellers even if they have their own e-commerce sites (more on e-commerce dilemmas in Secret 6). The corporate buyers of these entities are constantly hunting for better deals and better service. They spend considerable amounts of time searching the Internet.

So, let's imagine a corporate buyer in a manufacturing company is looking for a machine shop specializing in CNC (Computer Numerical Control) metal laser cutting. Such a buyer would type "CNC metal laser cutting services" into Google, and he/she would see a list of websites claiming to offer such services. Our buyer would most likely examine a couple of websites and select the one that looks the best, then he/she would call a number on that website or fill out a form. You just got found! Such requests for information (either via phone or a form) are called leads. That lead should be entered in your sales tracking system and handed to a sales rep to start a sales cycle.

Can I Afford It?

One additional wholesaler who finds you may mean a lot of business over the years. Ask yourself how much a new wholesaler is worth in profits over the next three years. I bet it's a large sum and probably in the tens or hundred thousands of dollars. So, just one additional distributor may pay for getting your website ranked high by the search engines!

If you are looking for the ultimate customers and not distributors, being found is relevant as well. This is especially true for any companies where the size of the transaction is relatively high. Examples include expensive services, such as environmental cleanup, large construction projects, legal services, and expensive machinery or goods. For such companies, even one new customer may pay for all the costs associated with a website that is optimized for search engines!

For most B2B companies, the investment in search engine optimization is very reasonable when compared to the value of new business generated by the Internet presence.

The investment made in your website stays with you and will be producing a stream of qualified leads for years to come. Given a very favorable return on investment (ROI), I consider this to be the least expensive way to expand your business.

As washing your hands is the single best way to avoid a disease, having a search engine optimized website is the single best investment in your digital marketing. A site that keeps catching the right buying signals will bring healthy profits to you for years to come!

HOW TO BE FOUND

- Discover how people search for your products/services and what phrases and keywords they type into search engines.

- Learn how often people search for your products/services. This will tell you about the demand for your offerings.

- Add one page per keyword to your website (landing pages).

- Make sure that a landing page has good content, easy to complete forms, and a prominently displayed phone number.

- Make sure that your website is mobile ready and displays well on smartphones and tablets.

CASE STUDY 1

Problem

A $20 million commercial printing company is facing a lot of competition in a shrinking industry. It wants to increase revenue by being found on the Internet. Here is the description of their services on their current website:

"We specialize in Corporate Communications • Fulfillment Services • Magazines • Catalogs • Folders • Direct Mail • Packaging & Labeling • Sales & Marketing Materials • Brand Identity • Training Materials • Graphic Design • Sheet-fed Offset Printing • Heat-set Web Printing • UV & Aqueous Coatings • Foil Stamping • Embossing • Inkjet Addressing • Poly Bagging • Mailing."

Solution

A digital marketing agency performed a keyword search using Google Keyword Planner. The analysis revealed the most popular searches when people were looking for printing services.

KEYWORDS	NUMBER OF MONTHLY SEARCHES
	(or the number of times people type in these phrases in Google)
brochure	4,400
screen printing	4,400
printing services	3,600
flyer	3,600
print	2,900
printing	2,400
poster printing	1,600
brochures	1,300
sticker printing	1,000
label printer	880
online printing	880
bookbinders	880

It became very obvious that the terms used on the website did not match the terms used when people searched for printing services. This is a very common occurrence. Business owners describe their products and services in their own terms without knowing how the general population refers to their services.

As a result of this analysis, the website content was changed to reflect the common keywords.

Result

Within three months, this website ranked on the first page of Google for five major keywords and resulted in over 50 qualified leads.

CASE STUDY 2

Problem

A global asset auction and liquidation service with offices worldwide assists large corporations with the liquidation of machinery equipment, including facilities, as well as industrial and commercial real estate. The majority of the visits to their site have been from purchasers looking to buy the assets available at their auctions. However, the company wants to find more customers worldwide who want to liquidate their assets. Each new customer who wants their assets liquidated is worth hundreds of thousands of dollars in profits to this company.

Solution

50 industry related phrases were identified for ranking in search engines. They were selected based on carefully researched phrases typed into the Google search engine over the last 12 months worldwide. For example, they included the following:

- **asset recovery**

- **company liquidation**

- **voluntary liquidation**

- **asset valuation**

- **asset sales**

- **machinery auctioneers**

- **liquidation companies**

New pages containing these keywords were added to the existing website. Each page adhered to 12 of Google's strict requirements on how to incorporate keywords in visible text as well as technical requirements behind the scenes.

Result

Within six months, the company ranked on 13 keywords on the first page of Google worldwide. As a result, the company has received over 10 requests for assistance in liquidation of multi-million dollar assets from around the world. Without the search engine optimization efforts, they would have never heard from these new potential leads. The profits from just one new customer found on the Internet paid many times more than the whole investment in this SEO project. It is hard to imagine a better return on investment.

SECRET 2
SCALE WITH MAIL
It's Not Your Grandfather's AOL

Email marketing has a bad rap. It's still perceived as low tech, the ugly duckling of digital marketing, and is associated with aggressive spam. All the glory and hype goes to social media. However, email marketing may be the second best investment you can make in B2B digital marketing.

Search engine optimization, as discussed before, was a pull technique. If done right, email is a very efficient tool to push your messages out.

Passport to the Internet

In the last 10 years, I've moved a lot. I've had four separate physical addresses in two different countries and have changed banks twice. As far as my digital identity, the only constant was my email address. It has travelled with me around the world, has been used as a user ID for many web-based services, including hotel and flight reservations, and has helped me stay in touch with friends, family, and business partners.

Email systems are much more than just a collection of messages. They are task lists, reminders, transaction confirmations, meeting schedulers, archives, and electronic journals going back many years. It's worth noting that the largest social media players use email extensively to promote their services. So, which one is more important? You can live without social media, but you cannot live without email.

LinkedIn offers a creative way to combine promotions via email based on the demographics of the targeted audience. For example, one can send a specific message using InMails only to professionals with "Sales Manager" title, in certain industries, in certain states and based on the specific size of company. This makes B2B advertising extremelly precise,

Our email addresses are, de facto, our Internet passports. Without an email address, we cannot exist in cyberspace.

Flexible, Customizable, Relevant

The best email marketing systems are surprisingly inexpensive. Most B2B companies can access a very sophisticated cloud-based system for less than $50 per month! And these systems are flexible and easy to customize. They come with many templates and allow for nice graphics, layouts, and a very professional look and feel. It is very easy to match the look and feel of your website with email graphics for branding consistency. Email programs are easy to use, and no programming knowledge is needed to get them going.

Segmentation, Upselling, and Cross-selling

Recipients can be segmented into many lists, and different messages can be sent to various people. So, for example, we may have a list of recipients who responded to promotion A and a list of those who responded to promotion B. We now can customize our message based on the recipient's preferences.

The same goes for lists based on previously purchased products. So, if we want to entice customers to buy different products based on their purchasing history, we can send them specific messages automatically.

The combinations are limitless but have to be well thought-out. In addition, modern email systems allow for rule-based automation. This means that we can automate sending various messages depending on recipients' demographics or behaviors as long as we have such data available in our database. We can send different messages to different distributors based on their profiles, for example.

Modern email systems provide forms that can be filled without having to switch to your website. So, we can put various calls to action in an email to make engagement as easy as possible. We can then analyze the effect of such promotions using email analytics.

Such flexibility, customization, and automation allows you to spread and track your messages in a very efficient manner.

Traceable and Accountable

One of the best features of email systems is the ability to track who opened an email. We call this an open rate and define it as a ratio of emails opened to those sent.

In addition, if we put links in our email, we can also track who clicked on these links and when. It's called a click through rate, and it is used to detect highly qualified prospects. We just assume that if individuals opened an email and clicked on the link in it, the message must have resonated with them. For example, a single email message may have multiple links for each of your products. If we notice more clicks for a certain product, it may flag a higher demand for that product.

Open rates and click through rates vary by industry, but each mailing campaign can be evaluated based on the performance of similar campaigns in the past. If any campaign varies substantially from a historical standard, it may require further analysis for poor performance. A poor email campaign performance usually is related to an ineffective email title or the lack of interest in your offer in general.

Emails are also great in customer service for routine notifications of status and transaction receipts, as well as opening and closing support tickets. I've creatively used email to update customers who applied for mortgages. Since the approval process is quite long and made up of various steps, customers have traditionally been kept in the dark for many days. Email automation allows a relevant status email to be sent every time a major milestone has been reached. Customer anxiety is diminished as well as the number of phone calls asking for the status. Win – win! The customer is happy, and you save time by not having to answer basic questions.

Engage Gradually, Tweak Constantly

Email campaigns can be tested on a very small scale by tracking and analyzing results. Since the cost of an individual campaign is very low, one can do a lot of "tweaking" to arrive at the best content.

In the digital marketing industry, this practice is called A/B testing. The principle is very simple but powerful: test message "A," then change a single element (such as the title, wording, color, or font). Call the new message "B" and compare both on rates of being opened and clicked through. With several attempts, one can come up with the optimal campaign content.

A Treasure Trove

Creatively using emails with existing customers can positively impact their retention. Existing customers have a tendency to open email from you, but they are less likely to visit your web pages. You can then use email to inform them about any new developments, products, or promotions. Use it for measuring their satisfaction. You can track what messages resonate better and what offers are more desirable by analyzing click through rates.

A good email list is also a great way to catch the attention of your potential customers and distributors. Each email may be a nice teaser with links to relevant pages of your website. Each email should allow for easy sharing on social networks as well as forwarding to friends. This technique can bring additional leads on top of leads generated by search engine optimization.

The Drip Effect

The best email campaigns are planned 12 months in advance to create a friendly "dripping effect." By law, email recipients have to be offered an option of removing themselves from any future mailings. Interestingly, this law contributes to the legitimacy of emailing as recipients feel that they have recourse against any undesirable email communication.

Ideally, your reps should have easy access to all the emails sent to existing customers as well as all prospects. This is easier said than done, and I will discuss the importance of systems integration in Secret 5.

THE POWER OF EMAIL

- Passport to the Internet

- Flexible, customizable

- Traceable

- Gentle dripping

- Upselling and cross-selling

- Customer service made simple

CASE STUDY

Problem

A metal industry company wants to sell more products to existing customers.

Solution

An email communication strategy has been formulated. The decision was made to email a newsletter from the president every 60 days.

To keep recipients opening, reading, clicking, and calling, the company creates good content with a passionate intro, lots of charts and graphs, new product announcements, industry news, and low-key promotions in the form of links introduced by phrases, such as:

- To speak to a live representative for quotes, click here

- To receive the most recent catalog for X, click here

- **To request more info, click here**

"Call me" links also lead to a page where visitors fill out a form indicating when they'd like to be called.

Result

On average, over 50 percent of recipients opened the email within the first two weeks. Website traffic jumped by 25 percent, and requests for live quotes improved more than 10 percent. In the end, more than 3 percent of existing customers completed the purchase of promoted items within six weeks of receiving that friendly email.

This company spends less than $100 per month on a cloud-based email marketing software system. The email content is generated in-house. This return on investment is very impressive, and the investment itself is very insignificant compared to other marketing efforts.

SECRET 3
24/7 SALES REP
WHO NEVER QUITS
A Digital Toolbox for Your Sales Force

A sales person will always be an integral part of any B2B company. Despite all the hype to the contrary, I cannot see a corporate buyer making a decision to buy a complex product/service without interacting with a knowledgeable sales rep. B2B selling is not like downloading music from iTunes. B2B products or services are too complex, too much prospect education is required, sales cycles are too long and political, and prices and terms require a salesperson's explanation. Quality sales reps in B2B are self-contained, miniature marketing departments. A good rep does branding, promoting, pricing, educating, negotiating, and customer service. This is why good B2B sales people make good money.

A Perfect Sales Rep

Have you ever met a sales professional who works 24/7/365, does not complain, ask for a raise, or need training, and fills out all the paperwork on time? That professional could be your website.

Today, most B2B websites are "electronic business cards." Just like their paper counterpart, they are necessary but hardly sufficient to generate leads and sales.

A Net for Catching Buying Signals

Imagine the following scenario: Your prospects easily find you on the Internet because your electronic business card has now changed to an active electronic prospecting net. The net catches leads from anyone who types your product name or service offering anywhere in the country (or the world).

When they land in the net – your website – they see a nice page matching their search. Impressed with the content and video testimonials, they call you or fill out an easy form. If they call, a phone conversation may be tracked or even recorded.

If they fill out the form, you just got another valid email address added to your mailing database. The leads keep coming 24/7/365.

In addition, all the subsequent technical questions from a prospect can be answered with videos, pictures, PDF spec documents, etc. So far, a real salesperson did not have to do much work.

Next, your real salesperson automatically gets all the information on the prospective customer in his or her CRM system. As sales cycles progress, your salesperson gets automatic emails or text when a prospective customer visits your website again. Such information includes pages they visited as well as time spent on each page. So, if they spent 90 percent of their time on a page describing Product A, and you offer 50 other products, it does not take a lot to discover the prospective buyer's real intentions.

Immediately, a salesperson can engage the buyer in a meaningful dialogue. But before doing so, he or she may want to learn as much about the buyer as possible.

Your Own NSA

According to Wikipedia, "The National Security Agency (NSA) is a United States intelligence agency responsible for global monitoring, collection, decoding, translation, and analysis of information and data for foreign intelligence and counterintelligence purposes." This definition of responsibilities reminded me of any decent sales competitive analysis – all of these tasks are performed on your market, competitors, products, distributors, industry trends, opinion leaders, customer satisfaction, and PR.

You cannot have all the listening power of the NSA, but you may be surprised how much valuable marketing information is flowing freely in cyberspace. It can be found on Twitter, LinkedIn, Facebook, Google+, Pinterest, and in electronic newspapers, magazines, and blogs.

The first challenge is the staggering amount of posts. How would you go about setting up a practical program for such monitoring/analysis?

Of course, you can go to any of the social media platforms and set up queries for certain keywords and hashtags. However, these platforms were not built for monitoring and analysis. They were designed for sharing a single piece of information with multiple recipients. Even if you had time to set up queries on all of these social media platforms, it would be time prohibitive to combine daily results in one comprehensive package.

Active Listening

There are several powerful but inexpensive systems on the market that allow sales reps to manage all this complexity in one well-configured package that can be integrated with your CRM. For example, sales reps can watch relevant social media posts grouped in the following "buckets" for active listening:

1. **Prospects**

2. **Competition – Companies**

3. **Competition – Products**

4. **Trade Shows**

5. **Industry**

6. **Opinion Leaders**

Thus, imagine having your own mini-NSA and catching anything relevant to your business from all the Internet chatter.

Monitoring Twitter can also provide a lot of insight, market research, and competitive info. It is now being used by industry leaders, major CEOs, and journalists. It's becoming a source of major industry news, and you can ignore it at your own peril. Before actively engaging in Twitter, I recommend simply monitoring it for three months. This will give you an idea of the appropriate level of your own activities in the future.

B2B Sales Reps Are Not Dead

I am not advocating replacing real salespeople with electronic ones. As I mentioned before, this will never happen in the B2B world. What I am advocating is supplementing the efforts of your highly talented and highly paid sales professionals with a 24/7 digital toolbox made of a hard working electronic net and a mini-NSA.

B2B sales talent is expensive, and the cost of replacing sales reps is very high. The best salespeople stay around only if they can make money. The average B2B sales rep makes well over $250K per year (including salary, commission, T&E, and management time). Therefore, before hiring another salesperson, you may want to consider equipping your existing sales force with the best digital sales toolbox possible. It will probably cost less than one year's salary for a single salesperson, and it will be "catching leads" and "snooping around" for years to come!

HOW TO HELP YOUR SALES REPS

- Catch buying signals with an electronic net

- Put leads in a CRM

- Set up active listening of social media

- Automatically analyze competition

- Automate customer support as much as reasonable

CASE STUDY

Problem

The existing website for a world-leading manufacturer of metal products was just an electronic business card and not effectively generating leads. The site was impossible to update without time-consuming efforts by website programmers.

Solution

After an in-depth analysis of various software vendors, the company decided to invest in an integrated lead generation system. With a new system, the marketing department gained better control over their website. They updated their old pages and easily created new ones. It was easy to create targeted content to capture leads online in new markets they never reached before.

Result

Within six months, they increased their website traffic by 600 percent and increased leads by 140 percent.

After capturing these leads through their new website, they tailored their follow-up correspondence to specific topics their leads were interested in (based on active listening). They tracked the leads in their CRM system. Within 12 months, they were able to prove to the management that the majority of all new customers came from their website.

SECRET 4
THE POWER OF
SIMPLICITY
Pamper Prospects and Customers with Elegant Simplicity

You have about four seconds to attract the attention of a new website visitor. If your website is perceived as irrelevant, the visitor will go to the competitor who is just one click away.

Easy Does It

Your website may be perceived as irrelevant because it has poor content, or most likely, because it is very hard to navigate, and/or it's slow to load. No matter what, the best content in the world is of no value if it is hard to reach.

Assuming that your website loads fast and has relevant content, it should be easy to navigate and interact with. Most visitors will abandon your site if they cannot spot a value in about five clicks.

Most visitors are spoiled by the simplicity of smartphones, tablets, 1-click ordering on Amazon, and first page results on Google. The search giant probably has the single simplest website in the world, generating billions in profits annually! If you think in terms of profit per number of user clicks, I cannot think of anything more effective or efficient. I know that Google is not a typical B2B company, but their website delivers on that point.

Five Clicks to Customer Retention

Most digital marketing press coverage relates to getting new customers. New customers, of course, are very important. It's equally critical to retain existing customers, keep them happy, and make upselling to them as easy as possible. Digital technologies may play a great role here.

You should strive to minimize the number of times a customer needs to click to interact with your business while reordering or seeking information. The ease of use is of paramount importance when facing prospective as well as existing customers.

Why Is It So Important?

If your customer support system is not easy to use, you will be spending a lot of time and money training and retraining your staff and your customers. Given the turnover on both sides, it can amount to a lot of money.

If your website is not easy to use, your customers will be calling your sales reps and customer support folks demanding immediate answers. That takes time away from selling. Ask yourself the following question: "What percentage of a sales rep's time is spent answering questions that could be answered by a well-designed website?"

If your website is not easy to use, you may be alienating your most important constituency – your existing customers. This will not help with retention and/or upselling efforts.

Do not burden your highly paid reps with having to answer basic questions, and do not annoy your customers by making them ask them.

Simplicity Is Complexity Resolved

Simplicity is not always easy to implement in customer service. Nevertheless, here are some tips:

- Reordering should be extremely easy with access to the history of previous orders. As a rule of thumb, it should be as easy as it is now when you reorder anything on Amazon.

- Provide easy access to all the reference materials (specs, price sheets, brochures, how-to videos, etc.). Good search functionality is a must.

- Product configuration forms should be intuitive.

- Email should be used extensively to alert, inform, and confirm any multistep processes spread over time.

- An easy to use ticketing system should be implemented for troubleshooting, complaints, and other complex tasks.

Last, but not least, you can use the ease of doing business with you as a selling feature.

THE POWER OF SIMPLICITY

"Simplicity is the soul of efficiency." —Austin Freeman

"Making the simple complicated is commonplace; making the complicated simple, awesomely simple, that's creativity." —Charles Mingus

CASE STUDY

Problem

An engineering firm was getting a lot of visits to their website but few visitors stayed for long and very few filled out the contact form or called the number listed there.

Solution

"Heat map" software was installed on their website to analyze where visitors clicked on a page. The concept of a heat map is simple but powerful. Analytical software allows a company to track the exact position of each click made by visitors.

Each click leaves an "XY coordinate footprint" on a page behind it. In other words, analytics will tell us that you clicked, for example, on the first page at the cross section of 678 pixels from the top and 460 pixels from the right.

The analysis revealed the following:

There were very few clicks on the landing page, which was full of small font text and lacked pictures. The contact form and phone number were at the bottom of a very long page and required a lot of scrolling to get to. Few visitors scrolled three screens down.

Of those who did, few filled out the form made of 10 required fields. The phone number was barely visible and listed at the very bottom of the page. The landing page was hard to use and to engage with.

Subsequently, the landing page was redesigned with the contact form and phone number displayed prominently at the top. The copy was rewritten to be much more concise with the key message placed above the fold – accessible without scrolling. Several relevant pictures were also added.

Result

The conversion rate (defined as the number of forms filled out compared to the number of visitors) jumped from 0.1 percent to 3.7 percent. The number of leads jumped from one per two months to four per week.

The lesson learned – try to make your marketing point above the fold of your page. This is not a new concept. Printed newspapers used to deliver top news above the fold, so it could be seen while folded in half and displayed on newsstands. The more things change, the more they remain the same.

SECRET 5
INTEGRATE OR
DISINTEGRATE

Data Integration Is Costly –
Lack of It Is Even More Expensive

Ask yourself what percentage of time your highly paid sales professionals spend on tasks that could be avoided altogether. My hypothesis is that it may be reaching 50 percent. The table below shows the common daily tasks of a typical B2B sales person.

ACTIVITY TYPE	SOFTWARE
Make a call	Log into CRM or spreadsheets
Take notes	CRM or spreadsheets
Send email	Email systems – Outlook, gmail, etc
Review prospect/customer internet activities	Visit multiple social media sites, Google Analytics, etc.
Engage on Twitter, LinkedIn, Facebook, etc. – research, posts, discussions, groups	Visit each social media site
Post to a blog	Visit/log to a blog
Write a proposal	Word processing software, presentation software, and document management software
Review orders, returns, sales volumes	ERP system
Status of open service tickets	Ticketing system
Take order	ERP system

It looks like up to 10 separate systems or websites may need to be accessed daily! So our salespeople are constantly logging in and out. Even with a single password, they have to jump between systems, keying in, rekeying, copying, and pasting.

Don't Keep Them In the Dark

In the end, it is still hard for sales people to analyze their own activities over time as the rekeyed data may not be kept in one place and/or may be in inconsistent formats. So, the analysis is time-prohibitive, and it's not being done, or it takes a lot of time and still may be compromised by the poor quality of manually entered data. This type of analysis usually takes place in a separate, private spreadsheet.

Many large companies have integrated activity logging for calls and email communications with clients and prospects. CRM systems do a great job at that, assuming that they are configured in the right way and do not overburden salespeople with too much bureaucracy.

Very few companies can provide a review of prospect or client Internet activities (including visits to internal web pages) inside CRM. Even fewer can provide a single interface for all of the above plus the ability to engage and track such engagements on social media. Ideally, as a salesperson, I would like to review all my calls, emails, social media posts, web visits, document downloads, pages visited, etc. from a single CRM interface. The importance of social media in selling is only growing, and it's not going away.

So far, we have been talking only about the selling side of activities; however, salespeople are also heavily involved in customer service. Thus, the ability to track actual orders, sales, and returns, as well as any open problem items cannot be ignored.

Some CRM systems allow for the integration of such support systems, but this is not an easy task depending on the vintage of the systems to be integrated.

DATA INTEGRATION

- Do you pay your sales reps for data entry?

- Integration of
  - CRM
  - ERP
  - Accounting
  - Social media
  - Web analytics

- Lack of integration is very expensive

CASE STUDY - THE HIDDEN COST OF COMPLEXITY

Let's assume that a salesperson costs a company $250K per year (salary, benefits, and commissions). If our hypothesis is true, then $125K goes into unproductive tasks that could be avoided with system integration. For 10 salespeople, you may be spending $1.5 million per year on manual data entry and analysis tasks instead of selling.

On an optimistic note, more and more systems are cloud-based and provide some standardization in terms of application interfaces. The older the system, the harder it is to integrate all the data. However, new companies have an opportunity to provide a high level of integration by stitching together a couple of existing cloud services with robust functionalities and relatively low monthly subscription fees. That will provide them with a cost advantage over older and larger players.

SECRET 6
TO E-COMMERCE
OR NOT TO
E-COMMERCE

Tips for Making Decisions About Creating an E-commerce Site

Many manufacturers of consumer products face the e-commerce dilemma: "Should we sell our products directly to consumers over our own e-commerce website?"

There are several temptations that come with e-commerce:

1. **Increased revenues**

2. **Higher margins**

3. **Direct contact with consumers**

4. **Keeping up with the digital Joneses**

Some disadvantages include:

1. **Cost of implementation and maintenance of a new e-commerce site**

2. **Shortage of e-commerce/Internet marketing skills**

3. **Possible conflict with existing distributors**

4. **Stiff competition from Amazon and, soon, Alibaba**

Before deciding whether to e-commerce or not, one should take several facts into consideration.

Despite all the hype and publicity, less than 7 percent of retail transactions in the U.S. are made over the Internet (based on sales volumes, not the number of transactions).

With this number in mind and everything else being equal, we should not expect any manufacturer of non-niche consumer products to sell more than 7 percent over the Internet. Shipping costs may have something to do with it. From the consumer perspective, buying on the Internet is not always less expensive.

Amazon Is Not Profitable Yet

For most non-niche products, there is stiff competition from Amazon, which has not made a profit since its inception despite humongous sales volumes and its purchasing and negotiating power. So, if Amazon cannot make money on e-commerce, how likely is it that an average manufacturer could?

There is also a lot of competition for rankings in Google for non-niche products. This means that it is hard to get these products to show up on the first page of Google. It's difficult even if you have top digital marketing professionals specializing in Google rankings (Search Engine Optimization – SEO) on staff. However, few manufacturers can afford to have this skill set on board. Thus, they engage digital marketing agencies to help them with e-commerce Google rankings.

Getting E-commerce Right Is Complex and Expensive

To put things in perspective, let's take a look at One Kings Lane, an e-commerce company that sells home décor and furniture but does not manufacture it. It has raised over $200 million in capital since its inception in 2009! As of last year, though, One Kings Lane was still unprofitable. (http://techcrunch.com/2014/01/30/in-the-quest-to-dominate-home-goods-e-commerce-one-kings-lane-raises-112m-at-a-912m-valuation/)

In summary, before jumping into e-commerce, a manufacturer may want to evaluate the above pros and cons. It may turn out that the best return on investment could be an extension of the distribution network. Thus, consider engaging a digital marketing agency to attract more distributors.

E-COMMERCE CHALLENGE

- Before you start,
    - check demand for your product – keyword search.
    - check competition for your keywords.

- Don't try to take on Amazon.

- Watch for conflict with existing distributors.

CASE STUDY

Problem

An e-commerce site delivers disappointing sales results after a considerable investment in time and money.

A water bottling company provides water with custom printed labels as well as private label services for several smaller chain stores in Southeast U.S. It also provides bottled water with custom labels for hotel chains, golf clubs, and sporting events.

Management has decided to go directly to customers via an e-commerce site. It made it possible for a customer to order as little as a case of water with a label designed on its website.

Six months after the e-commerce site launch, there were very few visits, the order sizes were really small, and customers complained about the problems with a complicated graphic design process. In addition, all the orders came from the same state where the factory was located.

Solution

Web traffic and competitive analysis was performed. The analysis provided several reasons for the disappointing results:

- **The company did not do keyword analysis and did not know that the volume of searches on Google for bottled water with custom labels in the Southeast U.S. was very small. Such an analysis would have halted this project at the beginning.**

- **There was competition online for custom bottled water solutions. It turned out that people could buy self-adhesive labels to be printed from their own computer. Such a label could then be wrapped over any bottled water by covering any existing labels.**

Again, the company did not do competitive research on Google or social media for alternative solutions already on the market.

- The cost of shipping water is very high in relation to the price of water itself. It was just not economical to ship water across many states.

Result

As a result of the above analysis, the e-commerce site was scrapped, including a graphical design interface, and the company decided to hire two full-time reps to call directly on restaurants, hotels, conference facilities, colleges, fitness centers, and other places that might be interested in large quantities of bottled water with their logo on it. The current website is no longer designed to attract individual purchases but to be found by institutions that might be interested in custom water products as part of their own branding.

SECRET 7
MEDIA OF MASS DISTRACTION

Sifting Through Facts and Fads –
Hype and Gripe of Social Media

Many B2B executives' attitude toward social media ranges between intimidation and irritation. After all, they've built successful businesses without having to worry about the Internet or a social media presence.

Should We Hire an English Major?

Nevertheless, given the overwhelming popularity of social media, I often see a typical reaction among B2B executives as follows:

"I think we need to be on social media. It looks like everyone else is. So, let's set up corporate LinkedIn and/or Facebook and/or Google+ and/or Twitter and/or Pinterest accounts and see what happens. Maybe we'll get some leads out of it. It's almost like a webpage – you have to have it."

So, they hire a twenty-something college graduate and put him or her in charge of social media on the assumption that millennials are proficient in these social communication tools (which they indeed are, but not necessarily in the business context).

Social Media ROI

A year or two later, there are no quantifiable results in increased sales attributable to spending a considerable amount of funds on such employees. The skepticism grows with respect to the value of social media. Where is the ROI? Intimidation turns to irritation.

The fact is that ROI for some social media activities can be proven but only with the right communication strategy and the right techniques.

On a strictly quantifiable front, one can measure ROI if the right links are placed at the right place within a social media post. The right link would lead back to the relevant page on a website.

So, if we are promoting Product A on Twitter (or anywhere else), we should include a link to *www.ourwebsite.com/productA* in a tweet (or Facebook post, etc.). Such a page, devoted to the promotion of Product A only via social media (also called a landing page), should have an easy-to-complete form and/or unique phone number associated with Product A. Then we can tally the number of forms filled out and/or the number of unique phone calls received and attribute these leads to social media campaigns. With the proper tracking, we can calculate the indisputable revenue that resulted from social media campaigns.

If we do not have the social media promotion and tracking set up right, even the best campaign can be disputed with respect to its effectiveness.

Should every post have such a link? Yes. I think you should strive for every promotional post having one. All such links should be abbreviated, so they do not take up too much real estate in the post. (On Twitter, it's virtually a requirement since most posts are limited to only 140 characters.)

Some posts will not have such links because we may be answering someone's questions, engaging in a discussion, or sharing someone else's content. However, there is nothing wrong with including them whenever it makes sense.

If we can prove a positive ROI for posts with links, all other posts will be "icing on the cake" – with the icing being our brand enhancement.

Listen Before You Engage

B2B companies should set up active listening systems before formulating social media policy. Social media will provide very few direct leads as compared to other channels such as SEO, paid ads, or email. However, managing social media can be a very time consuming process.

There are several tools on the market that can be set up as listening outposts as we described in Secret 3. Twitter is easily monitored and can provide a wealth of information on your industry, customers, and competitors. Twitter has become a publishing/PR platform used by industry thought leaders, CEOs, and top marketing officers of major companies. Combined with other tools for searching information on the Internet by keyword, it can provide invaluable market research insights. Based on several months of social media listening, it is much easier to decide to what extent it is going to play a role in your marketing mix.

Non-negotiable

You need some basic social media presence for two reasons:

- **It helps with search engine optimization (SEO) of your website.**

- **It's helpful to have professional looking corporate profiles on LinkedIn, Google+, and/or Facebook when a potential distributor/customer is checking you out.**

If you are going to use social media more extensively, select a few platforms and concentrate on doing a good job on them. Twitter plus LinkedIn or Facebook is probably just enough for a B2B company. Pinterest may be of value if you are manufacturing consumer products that look good in pictures. Educate yourself about how to use Twitter, set up communication policies, and roll out listening capabilities to your sales force, so they can have as much field intelligence as possible.

In summary, a B2B company will get greater benefits from using social media for market research and competitive intelligence as compared to engaging customers on it. Nevertheless, it will be hard to come up with an undisputable return on investment.

SOCIAL MEDIA

- **Have to be there but don't count on much business**

- **Hard to calculate return on investment**

- **Concentrate on just a few platforms**
  - **LinkedIn**
  - **Twitter**
  - **Google+**

- **Monitor before jumping in**

- **Use for competitive intelligence**

CASE STUDY

Problem

A distributor of electronic parts was deluged with all the information coming from social media on their competitors, partners, customers, and industry thought leaders. The management was not sure to what extent the company should be engaged on Twitter, LinkedIn, and Google+.

Solution

An off-the-shelf, cloud-based software program was installed to manage the competitive information. The software grouped social media posts in easy to create and access "buckets." For example, one can easily create a tab to store all information on any particular competitor, such as relevant social media posts based on keywords, hashtags, and brand names.

Result

A tweet from a marketing department of a competing company announcing a new product line was "caught" by the program and brought to the attention of the management. In the past, such information may have been learned many months later.

A tweet with complaints about the poor quality of customer service was also brought to the attention of management immediately. The customer was contacted, and the problem was solved on the spot, avoiding additional public relations issues.

SECRET 8
SCADS OF ADS
Is Online Advertising for You?

Google makes over 95 percent of their profits on $60 billion annual revenue (2014 figures) from online advertising. It also has about 65 percent of the market in the U.S. The rest is split between Yahoo and Bing. The business model is very simple yet very powerful. It is directly related to the tremendous power of very inexpensive telecommunication, storage, and analysis technologies. This business model would have not been viable even 15 years ago when computing power was just too expensive.

How Does It Work?

Let's say someone is looking for car insurance online and types "buy car insurance" into a Google search page. Google will list web pages for various insurance companies by matching keywords on their web pages with the term "buy car insurance." However, the top three positions on the first page are reserved for those insurance companies who paid Google to be listed there. The rest of the listings, called organic, are reserved for very well designed pages with great SEO implementations.

To get listed in the top three, a company pays Google when someone clicks on their listing. It is called Pay Per Click (PPC), and it's very attractive and precise as compared to, for example, print advertising whereby ads in the paper are shown to many people who are not in the market for car insurance.

How does Google decide the order among the top three? It is done by a live auction among advertisers. In simple terms, an advertiser tells Google that the most that they will pay is $3.00 per click. If anyone is willing to pay $3.20, that business will appear on the page above the lower bidder. The auction is open to anyone in the world.

A lot of dollars have been wasted in print advertising over the last 100 years. A popular saying illustrating how difficult it was to tie sales to print advertising is attributed to John Wanamaker, (1838–1922), a pioneer in advertising: "Half the money I spend on advertising is wasted; the trouble is I don't know which half."

Precise ROI and Great Market Research

Pay Per Click models allow for a very precise calculation of return on investment for advertising online. Google, Bing, or Yahoo provide detailed reports on the number of clicks and the overall cost of the campaign. The revenue and profit tied to a particular ad campaign can be determined from the internal accounting systems.

The reports break down ad expenditures by keywords. In other words, we can analyze whether the phrase "buy car insurance" performed better than "car insurance online" and then allocate the budget to the better performing phrases. So, not only is our online advertising very precise, it also provides us with market research insights leading to a more effective message on our websites.

The campaigns can be started and stopped at any time based on a set of criteria, such as desired time frames and/or budget availability.

Try Before You Buy

Online pay per click advertising needs to be evaluated case by case for each company. As a general rule, if you can demonstrate the desirable return on investment, it is worth advertising online.

A three-month pay per click test campaign can provide a lot of value and should not have to exceed a $3,000 budget. As we discussed before, one of the great benefits of digital marketing technology is that we can start gradually, test, measure, and come up with the optimal model that works for us. The following are the benefits of a three-month PPC campaign:

- **Discovering industry keywords that are performing best. This can be very valuable input for the content of future SEO efforts – it takes about six months to conclude the effectiveness of SEO. With PPC, we can find out what keywords to concentrate on earlier.**

- **Discovering what ad copy works the best. When our website is listed in Google, we have about 150 characters of text to entice visitors to click on our listing.**

- **Determining the size of the optimum budget. Spending too little on PPC may not get any results. Spending too much may not be effective either.**

- **Receiving actual leads and subsequent business that may pay for the test itself.**

PAID ADS

- **Try before you buy**

- **Discover the best keywords**

- **In the long run, less effective than good search engine optimization – SEO**

CASE STUDY

Problem

Owners of a startup company needed to go to market immediately and did not want to wait months for a professional SEO-ready website.

The startup company manufacturers roll-up industrial doors for large warehouses and production plants. Their compelling selling point is a lower price combined with better quality based on improvements in weight and insulation technologies. Their existing website was done cheaply by a relative who just graduated from high school. No search engine optimization best practices were applied. The site was not ranking at all on any of the relevant keywords.

Solution

They decided to hire a digital marketing agency to help them with paid ads to appear immediately. The agency performed a detailed search for all the relevant keywords and selected the most promising ones. A limited sample is presented below:

- **industrial doors**

- **roll-up doors**

- **roller shutter doors**

- **industrial roller shutter doors**

Result

Two weeks later, a campaign was in full swing with ads showing on the top of Google pages. The campaign was limited to a 100 miles radius from their manufacturing plant. In the first three months, they received over 30 qualified leads at about $80 per lead. Since then, they have closed six deals resulting in $12,000 profit and got a lead to a multi-location warehouse facility that may order several doors in the future.

The successful campaign achieved several objectives:

- **provided profitable leads**

- **provided information on the best industry keywords to be used in future SEO efforts**

- **provided input about the most effective ad copy**

- **provided information about the budget for a countrywide campaign that turned out to be cost prohibitive**

Based on the results of this campaign, two major digital marketing decisions were made:

- **build a new website optimized for searches countrywide**

- **eliminate paid ads gradually as the new website starts providing leads**

SECRET 9
ANALYTICS EQUAL
LESS POLITICS

If You Cannot Measure, Politics Creep In

One of the most exciting attributes and strengths of digital marketing is its transparency. We know about every visit and click (and even where our visitors clicked on the page). We know what geographic region they came from, what device they used, and which pages they visited on our website. What page they exited from and every page they visited is also available to us. We know how many times they downloaded our content, filled out a form, opened an email, or clicked on email links. If they purchased or returned products, we know. And we know how much they paid, too. In summary, we know their every digital interaction with our website, email campaign, and social media activities.

The Measurement Revolution

It is impossible (or impractical) to attribute increased sales to print and TV advertising.

Shooting from the hip in the past has been replaced with very precise targeting and monitoring. It was made possible because we can collect and analyze massive amounts of data at a very reasonable cost.

We are in the midst of a Measurement Revolution. Like any revolution, this one has its winners and losers. Losers may not even understand what hit them. The Measurement Revolution leads to increased productivity, better resource allocation, and less waste. Like any revolution, it is turbulent, uncomfortable, and challenges the traditional marketing order.

Inexpensive Tools

Software for web analytics comes free from Google. Information on who purchased what at what price comes from ERP (enterprise resource planning) and/or accounting systems.

These powerful and inexpensive analytics bring about several great benefits:

- **We can start our marketing gradually by testing various hypotheses and, subsequently, roll out very well-tuned marketing programs. This is true for SEO (just start with a couple of keywords), emails (testing various title lines and calls to action), testing the user friendliness of our website (heatmaps), paid ads (click through and conversion rates), and social media activities.**

- **We can come up with an optimal mix of activities among various channels for our overall marketing objectives based on the quantifiable return on investment. In other words, make a decision on how much to invest in SEO, email, paid search, and social media.**

- We can communicate undisputable, transparent results to management, thus minimizing guessing and managing by anecdote. The more we use analytics, the less likely we are to rely on politics when making decisions.

- We can set up quantifiable benchmarks to evaluate future campaigns.

- We can determine a more precise budget for future planning.

- As a result of all of the above, we can do more with less, thus improving the profitability of our operations.

ANALYTICAL - APOLITICAL

- The Measurement Revolution.

- Digital marketing results and processes are transparent.

- Marketing hypotheses can be objectively verified.

- Decisions are more effective and efficient.

- Resource allocation is optimized.

- If you can measure, you can manage.

CASE STUDY

The following table illustrates the ideal results of any digital marketing campaign. The actual numbers presented below are fictional, but they represent the most desirable relationships among them.

	VARIANCE	PLAN	ACTUAL
VISITS	3%	1,200,000	1,241,000
ENGAGEMENTS	9%	60,000	65,176
CONVERSIONS	19%	3,451	4,111
EXPENSES	-4%	$300,000	$287,000
REVENUE	15%	$567,989	$654,782
PROFIT	37%	$267,989	$367,782

The first line, *Visits*, represents the number of visits to our webpage. We have exceeded our plan by 3 percent. Our expectations were based on the previous campaign, but we wrote better copy for our listing that shows up in Google search results. Great!

The second line, *Engagements*, represents the number of visitors who engaged with our website for, let's say, more than one minute. (The definition of what constitutes engagement can be as simple as anybody who did not exit right away.) On average, the longer the visitor stays on our website, the better. Our expectations were exceeded by 9 percent because we posted more relevant content since our last campaign. This means that not only did we get more visitors than we expected, but more visitors stayed on our website longer than we expected (reading more). That's even better!

The third line, *Conversions*, shows the number of visitors who converted. Conversion is defined here as making a phone call to a number listed on the website, filling out a form, making a payment, downloading more information, or getting an answer via online chat. We exceeded our own plan by 19 percent because we supplemented the written content with product videos. This means not only that we attracted more visitors and engagements, but these engaged visitors did something that digital marketing is all about – they completed the journey that resulted in sales or leads (by leaving more information on how to reach them). That's the ultimate digital marketing dream!

However, to call this campaign a success, one needs to look at the return on investment (ROI). Here, we've achieved stellar results as well.

Expenses were lower than expected. How often does that happen? This may have been the result of some tasks done in-house instead of hiring outside help.

Revenue was 15 percent higher than we had promised due to more visits, more engagements, and more conversions.

Therefore, *Profit* exceeded our expectations by almost 40 percent!

As we mentioned before, the numbers for *Plan* and *Actual* are fictitious, but the relationships between them are feasible and desirable. Similar results presented here are the ultimate goal for any campaign (assuming that the *Plan* numbers were realistic). We did more with less expense, and we were able to prove it. How often does that happen?

Do You Know Where Your Profits Are?

Final remarks: the dashboard shown above looks very simple. Ideally, it should be available online in real time to enable quick reaction to any undesirable trends. In reality, it is quite hard to implement, as it requires integration of web analytics software (such as Google Analytics) with accounting software (assuming the right allocation of fixed and variable costs). Nevertheless, the table above represents the most desirable results with the best way of monitoring them.

In addition to the aggregated view illustrated here, such a dashboard should be automatically available for every channel (paid advertising, organic search, email campaigns, and social media sources) as well as basic known demographics (geography, device, age, income, etc.). Ultimately, you should be able to rank all the marketing programs/channels by their absolute as well as percentage profits.

Without an integrated system tracking the cost of marketing, sales, shipments, etc., it is very hard to figure out where the profits are coming from. Most companies are not equipped to track the profitability of their own digital marketing.

The devil is in the data. Data integration is expensive, but the lack of it may cost you even more.

THE INTERNET INDUSTRY

Major Players and Recent Trends

The rapid decrease in hardware, software, and telecommunication costs (as discussed in more detail in the Driving Forces chapter) enabled collection, movement, and storage as well as real time analysis of the massive amounts of data at a reasonable cost. The new Internet industry was born.

A Little History

Internet giants appeared from nowhere. In just 10 years:

- **Facebook signed up 1.2 billion users.[2]**

- **Google performs billions of queries daily.[3]**

- **GPS technologies track millions of movements at any moment.**

- **YouTube accepts millions of video uploads daily.[4]**

A Senior VP of Google Search shared the following 2012 statistics of his operations:

- **30 trillion unique URLs on the Web**

- **crawls 20 billion sites and processes a day**

- **3.3 billion searches per day**

These are staggering numbers indeed. They are so large that there was a need to come up with a new unit of measurement called a petabyte. A petabyte is defined as:

A **petabyte** (PB) is 10^{15} bytes of data, 1,000 terabytes (TB) or 1,000,000 gigabytes (GB)

- **It would take 223,000 DVDs (4.7GB each) to hold 1PB.**

- **Daily Internet traffic is around 700 PB.**

- **Facebook stores approximately 200 PB.**

Digital Advertising Is Born!

The rapid decrease in hardware, software, and telecommunications costs enabled business models whereby Internet services are free, but the cost of running the service is covered by digital advertising to a very large population. This model has no precedence in human history. Advertisers are excited about the increased effectiveness of the new channel and don't mind bankrolling the new model. They can stretch their advertising budgets and get a much better measurement of their marketing effectiveness.

Phones Became Smart

There are around 200 million smartphones in the U.S. [6] Each one is a powerful computer with a GPS. They quickly became indispensable by connecting people to the Internet. As a result, 34 percent of all searches today begin on smartphones, and 65 percent of emails are opened on smartphones. [7,8]

If a new local business does not have a mobile presence on the Internet, it is unlikely to succeed.

To Find and Be Found

With a staggering amount of data available, it was a challenge to make it useful. Without an effective way to sift through all of it, the information was of little value if it could not be found.

In response to this challenge, search engines were created. They have addressed both sides of the same coin: how can I find a product, service, business I am looking for, and also, how can my product, service, or business be found on the Internet by potential buyers?

In order to be found, the websites had to signal their content to search engines. Thus, search engine optimization techniques (SEO) were adopted. SEO allows for a match to be made between search terms typed into a search engine and the content on a website.

Being Found Is Not Enough

Finding a website is the first step in finding good information. A search engine may produce a list of many sites that match our search criteria. This does not mean that the content of these sites is of value. Actually, too many sites are poorly designed, hard to use, misleading, and very, very slow.

The rules for finding and being found on the Internet are as simple as ABC. First, we have to **Attract** a visitor to show up in the search results listing. We do that by placing the right keywords on our pages – keywords and phrases that will match the items being searched.

Next, we have to **Bring** the potential visitors to our site. We have about 210 characters to do that. Our listing will have the address of our website and the corresponding description. If our address and/or description are poorly worded, misleading, and/or missing, it is unlikely that our link will be clicked on. On the other hand, if they match the expectation of a person doing the search, that person will most likely click on our listing.

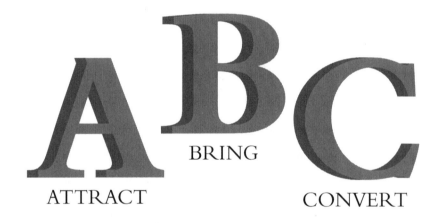

ATTRACT BRING CONVERT

Last, but not least, we have to **Convert** a visitor to either a customer or qualified prospect. If we are running an e-commerce site and a visitor completed the purchase after landing on our website, we can claim total victory along our ABC continuum. Another desirable result would be a phone call to a sales rep and/or a form filled out with a request for more info.

Major Players

The table below lists all the major Internet players. On the list, there are hardware and software companies, telecommunication giants, and e-commerce titans. They are involved in many vertical industries listed across the top.

It's worth noting that only Google covers the full range of products. Each of the companies listed here are jockeying for positions in various verticals, and there is a lot of competition at the top.

COMPANY	BROWSER	HARDWARE/OS	MUSIC	VIDEO
Apple	+	+	+	
Alibaba			+	
Samsung		+		
Google	+	+	+	+
Facebook				
LinkedIn				
Pinterest				
Microsoft	+	+		
Yahoo			+	
Amazon			+	
Twitter				

COMPANY	E-COMM.	SEARCH	SOCIAL	PAID ADS	APPS
Apple					+
Alibaba	+	+	+	+	+
Samsung	+				+
Google	+	+	+	+	+
Facebook	+	+	+	+	+
LinkedIn		+	+	+	
Pinterest		+	+	+	
Microsoft		+		+	+
Yahoo		+		+	
Amazon	+	+		+	
Twitter			+	+	

Summary

- Google is facing search competition from Amazon and aggregators, such as Yelp, Manta, and wow.com.

- Facebook, Amazon, LinkedIn, and Pinterest all offer paid ads.

- Amazon (which is still not profitable) will be facing a profitable Alibaba.

- Microsoft is not a major force outside of Office products (Remember how we were afraid of Microsoft in the past?).

- Facebook has the largest number of users on mobile apps (this includes Instagram).

- Mobile advertising is growing fast, and Facebook sells more mobile ads than Google. [12]

- Google has 63 percent market share in searches from desktops, 92 percent from mobile/tablets.[13]

- Google, Apple, and Microsoft have their own browsers.

- Google controls Android – the operating system for the majority of smartphones in the world.

Conclusions

- Apple, Google, Facebook are here to stay.

- Social media will see fads come and go with the up-and-comers being acquired by today's titans.

- Android and iOS are here to stay with Android appealing to the lower end of the affluence spectrum.

- **The Internet will generate even more data to be stored, analyzed, and monetized. Examples include Apple Watch, iBeacon for tracking in-store foot traffic, and Google Nest thermostat.**

As seen on the graph below, some of the major players are huge business entities. Apple is the most valuable company in terms of market capitalization. It's ahead of traditional giants, such as ExxonMobil, Johnson & Johnson, and Walmart. Microsoft and Google are not far behind.

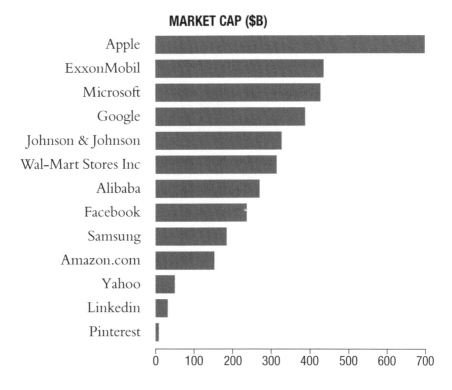

MARKET CAP ($B)

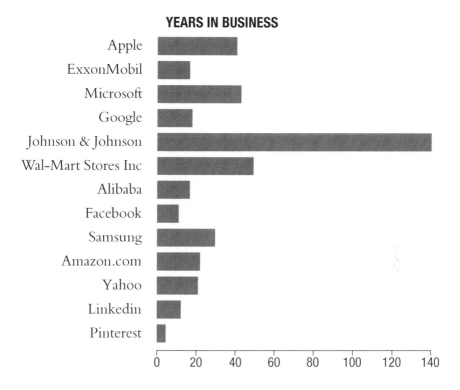

YEARS IN BUSINESS

To put these numbers in perspective, the annual revenue of Apple is equal to the annual GDP of the whole country of Ecuador. Amazon is comparable to Kenya, Yahoo to Mongolia, and Microsoft to Croatia.

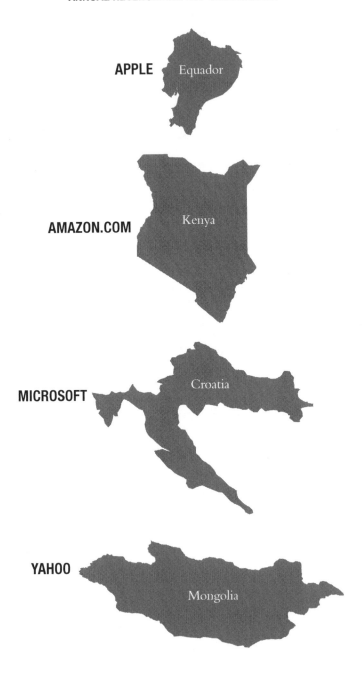

RECENT TRENDS

Smartphones

Samsung's smartphone sales over the 2014 holidays were somewhere between 71 million and 75 million —putting it roughly on par with Apple, which sold a record 74.5 million iPhones over the same period. [14]

A good mobile presence is a must because mobile payments are around the corner, and our phones will become our digital wallets.

The Home Depot has announced it will spend $1.5 billion to improve its supply chain and other back-end systems related to mobile ordering. [18]

Hilton Worldwide is investing $550 million to serve its guests in their mobile moments and transform its entire customer experience.[18]

Video Marketing

Videos are a must-have as well. YouTube is the second largest search engine next to Google. Videos also are easier to get ranked for and have a higher click through rate. The younger audience is more accustomed to video formats.

Content, Content, Content

Good content is increasingly important. There are two interconnected reasons for that. First, search engines reward good content as it is in their best interest to list only websites with good quality. Second, good content increases the chances for visitors engaging, sharing, and converting.

E-commerce

Despite all the media attention, e-commerce in the U.S. accounts for only 6.6 percent of retail sales in terms of dollars spent. Yes, many people are shopping online and that number is increasing; however, they tend to buy smaller items and products that are easy to ship at low rates.

To put things in perspective, as mentioned earlier, Amazon is not profitable yet [15] despite its enormous scale and buying power. On top of that, the profitable and equally powerful e-commerce Chinese company Alibaba is entering U.S. market. I expect a lot of price competition between these two giants. This does not bode well for B2B e-commerce, especially for commodity type products.

E-commerce combined with brick and mortar stores brings about another marketing challenge, which is the multi-channel buying journey. People start shopping at home on their desktop or tablets then go to a store to do additional comparisons and then buy in-store or via smartphone, depending on prices and terms. If a store visitor opts for in-store tracking, special offers will be pushed to their phones while they shop. This is a B2C phenomenon; nevertheless, it illustrates how smartphones impact marketing and retailing.

Our TV Watching Habits

"By 2018, Internet advertising will be poised to overtake TV as the largest advertising segment." [16] According to Nielsen, YouTube reaches more U.S. adults aged 18–34 than any cable network.[17]

Our watching habits are changing. We are slowly shifting to streaming services like Netflix or Pluto TV. Paying over $100 per month for 500 channels of cable (of which we watch less than 10) does not seem like a sustainable model going forward.

Search Challenge

Search engines face an interesting challenge. It turns out that 16 to 20 percent of queries that get asked every day have never been asked before. [3]

This is driven by how our language is changing as well as how questions are asked. For example, we search differently on phones (by speaking) than when typing on a keyboard.

Search engines are still returning too many irrelevant listings, and the special aggregators are addressing this frustrating issue.

Aggregators

Google is not immune to competition. We are observing the increasing power of aggregators who include valueable reviews. Yelp, Manta, Angie's List, and to some extent LinkedIn, are just a few examples.

With the exception of local listings, search engines do not provide access to company testimonials. These recommendations are getting increasingly important for online branding.

In B2B, Manta provides useful information on company size and executive bios. When sales reps prepare to call on company X, visiting Manta and LinkedIn may provide more relevant information in less time when compared to a Google search.

Summary

- Rate of technological change will not slow down.

- Combining creative, analytical, and technical aspects is important. Few individuals combine them all – those who can will come at a high premium.

- There is more data, tracking, and analysis available today.

- **The need for online analytics will drive data integration.**

The following skills will be in high demand and/or short supply:

- **Copywriters and copy editors**
- **Multimedia experts – especially with video skills**
- **Business analysts – marketing and IT go-betweens**
- **Data analysts – drawing conclusions and formulating actions**

For most B2B companies, it will be very hard to attract and keep this type of talent. As a result, there will be high demand for assistance from digital marketing agencies.

References

1. http://www.techpolicydaily.com/communications/much-iphone-cost-1991/
2. http://thenextweb.com/facebook/2014/01/29/facebook-passes-1-23-billion-monthly-active-users-945-million-mobile-users-757-million-daily-users/
3. http://www.internetlivestats.com/google-search-statistics/
4. https://www.youtube.com/yt/press/statistics.html
5. http://www.dailymail.co.uk/sciencetech/article-2247081/There-soon-words-data-stored-world.html
6. http://www.statista.com/statistics/201182/forecast-of-smartphone-users-in-the-us/
7. http://www.pewinternet.org/fact-sheets/mobile-technology-fact-sheet/
8. http://venturebeat.com/2014/01/22/65-of-all-email-gets-opened-first-on-a-mobile-device-and-thats-great-news-for-marketers/
9. https://www.google.com/
search?q=market+capitalization+of+google&oq=market++capi-talization+of+google&aqs=chrome..69i57j0l5.11910j0j4&-sourceid=chrome&es_sm=91&ie=UTF-8
10. www.wikipedia.org
11. http://www.businessinsider.com/25-corporations-bigger-tan-countries-2011-6?op=1
12. http://www.businessinsider.com/mobile-is-growing-faster-than-all-other-ad-formats-2014-10
13. https://www.netmarketshare.com/search-engine-market-share.aspx?qprid=4&qpcustomd=0
14. http://recode.net/2015/01/28/apple-and-samsung-in-dead-heat-for-smartphone-dominance/
15. http://ycharts.com/indicators/ecommerce_sales_as_percent_re-tail_sales

16. http://www.cmocouncil.org/facts-stats-categories.php?view=all&-category=marketing-spend
17. https://www.youtube.com/yt/press/statistics.html
    http://blogs.forrester.com/thomas_husson/14-11-11-mobile_lead-ers_will_break_away_from_laggards_in_2015

9 B2B DIGITAL MARKETING AND SALES MANAGEMENT TIPS

1. It's all about the qualified leads.

At the end of the day, marketing has only one purpose: to deliver **qualified** leads to your sales people. If you flood your sales force with unqualified leads, they will stop paying attention to your marketing efforts.

2. Involve sales managers from the start.

Digital marketing projects are not only technically complex. They require a great deal of cooperation between marketing and sales. Make sure that any digital marketing project starts with representatives of your sales organization. In many smaller organizations, B2B salespeople are self-contained mini-marketing departments, and they have a wealth of knowledge about your market, competitors, products, etc.

3. Start with a 12-month digital marketing plan.

Digital marketing projects tend to be complex and involve multiple players, steps, and deliverables. Make sure you plan ahead with a well-structured road map that is easy to communicate to all involved.

4. Be patient and manage expectations.

Digital marketing is about the constant verification of various hypotheses. It is about constant measurement and analysis. It is very unlikely that there will be conclusive positive results in less than 6–12 months. It takes time to prime the "digital pump" before a steady flow of leads begins.

Make sure that major decision makers have realistic expectations about the timeframe for expected results.

5. Define how you are going to know you succeeded.

Any digital marketing effort should include measurable goals that all parties agree to. One of the many advantages of digital marketing is the transparency of analytics. The progress against goals should be analyzed and shared at least monthly.

6. Set up digital lead tracking.

If you have lead tracking in place, make sure that leads that originated from your digital marketing are marked as such. Sales cycles in B2B may exceed 12 months, and nobody will remember a year from now where the leads came from if they were not properly tracked.

If you already have a CRM, tag the leads appropriately. If you do not have a central place for lead tracking, seriously consider implementing it.

Without effective lead tracking, it will be impossible to assess how much business resulted from your digital marketing efforts.

7. Combine traditional with digital.

You have built a successful business with traditional marketing and sales methods. Keep doing what has worked so far: word of mouth, trade shows, print ads, direct sales, etc.

However, come up with a plan about how to supplement the traditional methods with new digital tools. Principles of marketing and sales have not changed, but let's take advantage of the new technologies that make lead generation and selling more effective and efficient.

8. Team up with the pros.

It is unlikely that the average B2B company would have employees with the skill set required to set up a digital marketing program. Such talent is hard to find, hard to retain, and comes at a premium.

Team up with an experienced B2B digital marketing agency. As a part of due diligence, ask for case studies of projects they have completed for other B2B companies. These studies should contain real analytics from the implementations – the best proof being screenshots from Google Analytics programs showing the actual traffic and lead numbers as well as ranking on the keywords.

9. Before you hire an additional sales rep ...

Equip the existing sales force with digital tools by implementing CRM that provides a steady supply of qualified leads and set up social media intelligence monitoring and engagement as well as real time notification of website visits by major prospects. The cost of setting up digital marketing may be less than hiring a new salesperson.

18 TIPS FOR YOUR WEBSITE

In the past, traditional marketing did not require attention to real time technological details. Modern digital marketing campaigns rely on creative content as well as mundane, unglamorous technicalities. A multi-million dollar campaign can be ruined by such trivial things as the website not loading fast enough or links leading to the wrong places.

Your website is the single most important component of your Internet presence. So, here are 18 tips to make sure your website has all the critical components.

1. Speed

It if takes more than four seconds to load your site, you will most likely lose visitors. It is of utmost importance to assure quick load times.

2. Mobile Presence

If your website displays poorly on mobile devices, you may be penalized in mobile Google searches (as of April 21, 2015). The percentage of Internet traffic originating on mobile devices exceeds 40 percent, and it's still growing. If you are not visible on mobile devices, you may be missing a lot of visits.

3. Broken Links

There is nothing more annoying to visitors (and embarrassing to website owners) than broken links (like when they lead to "Page Not Found" or other irrelevant content). Make sure there are no broken links anywhere on your website.

4. Readability

Websites should be written at an 8th grade level. If your website is written in a complex language requiring a high level of proficiency, it will turn off the majority of the population. The site has to be easy to read and navigate.

5. Analytics

Analytics allow you to track each visit, duration of stay, clicks, downloads, etc. This information is critical for every website. Technically, each page on your website need to be enabled for analytics. If some pages lack this functionality, it will be impossible to get a full picture of your website performance.

6. Printability

Printing is still a very popular way to get, store, and share information. Make sure that your site is easily printable on standard page sizes. Printable stylesheets should be used. They allow for extensive control over the printed version of a webpage. For instance, removing navigation and adjusting the layout to fit. Ease of use for your visitors is of the utmost importance.

7. Search Ranking

Once a month, check the ranking of your keywords in major search engines. Your rankings will fluctuate depending on your efforts as well as the competition.

8. W3C Standard Compliance

W3C compliance is an international standard for measuring website code quality and browser compatibility. Lack of compliance may result in poor displays in various browsers, such as Safari, Chrome, Explorer, or Firefox.

9. Keyword Analysis

Check how frequently your keywords occur in your website's content. Let's assume that you are trying to rank in Google with the phrase "red boots." Make sure that this phrase does not occur too frequently on your pages.

10. Duplicate Content

Make sure that your content is original and not a copy of somebody's else work. Do not repeat identical content on multiple pages of your website either. Copyright violations are easy to detect, and search engines penalize duplicate content even if it's your own.

11. Social Interest

Check to see how many social networks your content is being shared on. It may tell you what particular information from your website is the one most referred to.

12. Page and Word Counts

The number of words per page should not exceed 1,000. Lengthy copy is rarely read and contributes to a feeling of clutter.

13. Incoming Links

Work on increasing the number of sites that link to your website. Generally, the more links to a website, the higher it will rank in search engines. Good websites will tend to accumulate links naturally over time. Links from educational or governmental websites are highly desirable.

14. URL Format

Poor URL formatting has many implications: webpages are less likely to appear highly in search engines, are harder to exchange socially, and are confusing for users. URLs can be improved by using technology like URL rewriting, without needing to completely replace the existing code. For example, your URL may read www.mycompany.com/new-products, or it may have a much more confusing version, such as www.mycompany.com./?_escaped_fragment_=about-us/c10th.

15. Alternative Text

All your images should have alternative text with a relevant keyword. The alternative text shows up when a mouse hovers over an image. This is important for two major reasons. It helps people with visual disabilities and helps with search engine rankings.

16. Headings

Make sure that you correctly define headings. It is particularly important for search engine optimization as well as content readability.

17. Open Graph

Open Graph tags tell social networks how to share content of a website. Using them correctly makes the shared content format and display properly on social networks. This, in turn, leads to the increased likelihood that the content will be shared.

18. Contact Details

Make sure that phone numbers and postal addresses are present and visible, and that there is no conflicting information. Your visitors should not have trouble finding the right number and address.

CONCLUSION
My Call to Action for You

I have written this book to provide unbiased, "straight-talk" jargon-free, no buzzwords advice to B2B executives who wonder if digital marketing is for them or where to start their digital marketing project.

The world of digital marketing can be confusing mostly due to the endless deluge of new and less expensive technologies hitting the market.

I consider an investment in digital marketing as the least expensive way to grow sales. A well-executed digital marketing strategy may lead to a 10–15 percent increase in sales. This can be brought about with a very reasonable investment, which usually costs less than hiring a single salesperson.

I have two valuable offers for you:

The first is FREE EVALUATION of your organization's digital marketing capabilities and the other is a FREE ONE HOUR CONSULTATION.

For the FREE EVALUATION, please go to www.b2bdigitalmarketingsecrets.com. You will find there a Digital Marketing Readiness Test. This is an assessment of the maturity of your Internet presence.

The results of this objective evaluation will help you to formulate and prioritize your digital marketing strategies. It will also help you with budgeting as well as selling your marketing programs to your peers and managers.

For your FREE CONSULTATION contact us at (904) 834-1490 or by email at consulting@b2bdigitalmarketingsecrets.com.

INSPIRATION

I love quotes and the accumulated condensed wisdom of the best human minds. The following are my favorite quotes related to marketing, sales, and technology.

"Computers are incredibly fast, accurate and stupid; humans are incredibly slow, inaccurate and brilliant; together they are powerful beyond imagination." —Unknown

"New technology is common, new thinking is rare." —Sir Peter Blake

"Everybody gets so much information all day long that they lose their common sense." —Gertrude Stein

"Getting information off the Internet is like taking a drink from a fire hydrant." —Mitchell Kapor

"Turn off your email; turn off your phone; disconnect from the Internet; figure out a way to set limits so you can concentrate when you need to, and disengage when you need to. Technology is a good servant but a bad master." —Gretchen Rubin

"We must move from numbers keeping score to numbers that drive better actions." —David Walmsley

"It's much easier to double your business by doubling your conversion rate than by doubling your traffic." —Jeff Eisenberg

"The success of your web page should be measured by one criteria: Does the visitor do what you want them to do?" —Aaron Wall

"People ignore design that ignores people." —Frank Chimero

"Sometimes when you innovate, you make mistakes. It is best to admit them quickly, and get on with improving your other innovations." —Steve Jobs

"Data beats opinion." —Unknown

"Twitter is a great place to tell the world what you're thinking before you've had a chance to think about it." —Chris Pirillo

"If you make customers unhappy in the physical world, they might each tell 6 friends. If you make customers unhappy on the Internet, they can each tell 6,000 friends." —Jeff Bezos

"In the long history of humankind those who learned to collaborate and improvise most effectively have prevailed." —Charles Darwin

"There is nothing so useless as doing efficiently that which should not be done at all." —Peter Drucker

"Facebook did not exist; Twitter was a sound; the cloud was in the sky; 4G was a parking place; LinkedIn was a prison; applications were what you sent to college; and Skype for most people was a typo. All of that changed in just the last six years." —Thomas Friedman

ABOUT THE AUTHOR

Greg Gutkowski is a highly sought after Internet marketing strategist who is in demand by many of the world's most successful companies. Greg's global experience includes prior work as co-founder of Efekt Technologies, a European Internet software company where he was responsible for building a multi-lingual marketing and sales team. He was also founder of just5clikcs, Inc. a company specializing in data analysis and business intelligence services.

His 20 years of multidisciplinary business experience includes digital marketing, sales, and IT management as well as Internet software development. Over the years Greg has worked with such major players as Allstate, American Express, Aon, AT Kearney, AT&T, Blue Cross Blue Shield of Illinois, Charmer-Sunbelt, Dean Foods, First Bank, Hewitt, IBM, Mobil Oil, Northern Trust, Penn Mutual, Ralph Lauren, and United Stationers.

Greg is passionate about information technologies and data analytics driving profitable marketing and sales processes. He has earned the following advanced degrees: MBA in IT Management, MS in Economics and a MS in Journalism.

His website is www.b2bdigitalmarketingsecrets.com

Connect with Greg on LinkedIn at:
https://www.linkedin.com/in/greggutkowski

Made in the USA
San Bernardino, CA
01 June 2018